T0011822

the little book of
NUMEROLOGY

Published in 2024 by OH!
An Imprint of Welbeck Non-Fiction Limited,
part of Welbeck Publishing Group.
Offices in: London – 20 Mortimer Street, London W1T 3JW
and Sydney – Level 17, 207 Kent St, Sydney NSW 2000 Australia
www.welbeckpublishing.com

Compilation text © Welbeck Non-Fiction Limited 2023
Design © Welbeck Non-Fiction Limited 2023

Disclaimer:

This book and the information contained herein are for general
educational and entertainment use only. The contents are not claimed to
be exhaustive, and the book is sold on the understanding that neither the
publishers nor the author are thereby engaged in rendering any kind of
professional services. Users are encouraged to confirm the information
contained herein with other sources and review the information
carefully with their appropriate, qualified service providers. Neither the
publishers nor the author shall have any responsibility to any person
or entity regarding any loss or damage whatsoever, direct or indirect,
consequential, special or exemplary, caused or alleged to be caused, by
the use or misuse of information contained in this book.

All rights reserved. No part of this publication may be reproduced,
stored in a retrieval system, or transmitted in any form or by any means
(including electronic, mechanical, photocopying, recording, or otherwise)
without prior written permission from the publisher.

ISBN 978-1-80069-198-8

Editorial consultant: Katalin Patnaik
Editorial: Victoria Denne
Project manager: Russell Porter
Production: Jess Brisley

A CIP catalogue record for this book is available from the British Library

Printed in China

10 9 8 7 6 5 4 3 2 1

the little book of
NUMEROLOGY

9 7 5 3
4 3

katalin patnaik

OH!

CONTENTS

INTRODUCTION

Humankind has had a fascination with numbers since the beginning of time.

Each culture has its own numbers that have special significance for them, be that for good or bad reasons.

The reason behind numbers being lucky or unlucky is deeply embedded in the specific culture.

In Europe and North America, the number 13 is considered unlucky. This is said to have its roots in Norse mythology, when Loki gatecrashed a funeral, bringing the number of gods up to 13, and all hell broke loose.

Similarly, Judas, who betrayed Christ and led to his crucifixion, was also thought to be the 13th guest at the Last Supper.

The number 4 is seen as unlucky in Japan and China because it sounds like the word for death.

So strong is their fear that there will often be no fourth floor in buildings such as hotels, apartment blocks and hospitals, and the elevator buttons will skip straight from 3 to 5.

When written with Roman numerals, Italy's own unlucky number 17 (XVII) can be rearranged into VIXI, meaning "I am dead".

Numerology takes the significance of numbers further than luck and, using an alphanumeric system, whereby each letter of the alphabet is assigned a number, studies the numerical value of words and names.

From this, one can find patterns and divine meaning.

For example, an inscription from 8th-century BCE Assyria states:

"the king Sargon II built the wall of Khorsabad 16,283 cubits long to correspond with the numerical value of his name."

Ancient Sumerians, Egyptians,
Arabians and Chinese all had their
systems to harness the mystical
power of numbers.

As a result, there are many different
traditions of numerology.

In this book we will discuss the Pythagorean method that is most well-known to the West.

Other popular methods include the Agrippan method, the Chaldean method, and Jewish gematria.

so what is

PYTHAGOREAN NUMEROLOGY
and HOW DOES IT WORK?

As its name suggests, Pythagorean numerology was developed by Pythagoras, the ancient Greek philosopher.

You might remember his name from maths class, when learning about the Pythagorean Theorem.

He and his followers believed that everything was part of a system, a well-thought-out order that is reflected in the orderliness of numbers.

Each number has a specific meaning that encompasses number's unique characteristics.

Each number has a specific meaning that encompasses number's unique characteristics.

For example, the number 1 means the first thing, the start of something.

The first step on a journey often requires the biggest effort, and when we come first in a competition, that is because of our hard work.

From this, it is easy to see how
the meaning of 1 becomes about
determination and drive.

Because everything in this Universe
is interconnected and planned out,
Pythagoras believed that the time
at which we were born and the
names we were given are not
accidental, either.

These aspects of our being reflect our soul, the energy we came here with, as well as the challenges and goals we will encounter in our lives.

Numerology helps us decipher this information so we can make the most of our journey on this plane of existence.

Even though everything is planned out and works within a system, this does not mean the future is set in stone.

Numerology is best suited for self-exploration, but it can also be used to take a peek into the future – keeping in mind that what we see is the *potential* of something happening, not necessarily what *will* happen.

Because you have free will, your decisions and actions can create a different outcome to what was originally going to happen, and forces outside your control can be at play as well.

The good news is, even if you are not very good at maths, you can still be amazing at numerology.

The most difficult calculations you'll have to do are basic additions and subtractions. It is absolutely manageable.

All you need is your date of birth, your name, a pen and paper, and you are ready to build up your chart.

CHAPTER

GETTING STARTED

In numerology, each letter is assigned a **single-digit number**, based on its position in the alphabet.

We start with **1**, and the biggest number we use is **9**.

Using the chart opposite, we calculate the numbers of the letters in our name, using the methods given in this chapter.

Let's see an example.

1	A	J	S
2	B	K	T
3	C	L	U
4	D	M	V
5	E	N	W
6	F	O	X
7	G	P	Y
8	H	Q	Z
9	I	R	

To calculate a name's **Expression Number**, we need to find the value of every letter used in the name, then add them up.

So, when we add up all the letters in the name "Elizabeth", we get the number 43, like so:

E	L	I	Z	A	B	E	T	H
5	3	9	8	1	2	5	2	8

$5 + 3 + 9 + 8 + 1 + 2 + 5 + 2 + 8 = \mathbf{43}$

We are always aiming to end up with a single-digit number, so from there we would add up the two digits of '43' (4 and 3) to get 7.

$$4\,3 = 4 + 3 = \mathbf{7}$$

Elizabeth's **Expression Number** is **7.**

Remember, this is only an example to illustrate how to do the calculations.

We almost always use people's full names when doing a proper analysis.

In numerology, we do not consider how a letter is pronounced, or, indeed, whether it is pronounced at all.

We simply calculate the value of each letter just as the name is written down.

The only tricky letter is Y.

There will be times when we calculate the numerical value of only the consonants or only the vowels in a name.

Here, the rule is: if a Y sounds like a vowel, for example in Yvette, Lynn or Mary, then it is considered a vowel. Where it has a soft J sound, such as in Yasmin, then it is considered a consonant.

CHAPTER

2

CALCULATING CORE NUMBERS

the LIFE PATH
number

This number is the most important one of all.

It shows the blueprint, the script of our life, with all the lessons, obstacles and chances we will encounter on the way.

To calculate your **Life Path Number**, you simply have to add up the day, month, and year of your birth.

To allow special numbers to emerge, you need to first reduce each component of the date to a single digit, then add them all up.

Let's take the famous English king who had six wives, Henry VIII, as an example. His birthdate is

28 June 1491

which, when we put it numerically, becomes

28 06 1491

Now, we add each set of numbers (the day, the month, then the year) up until each one is a single digit.

So: 28 becomes

$$2 + 8 = 10, \text{ then } 1 + 0 = \textbf{1}$$

06 becomes

$$0 + 6 = \textbf{6}$$

1491 becomes

$$1 + 4 + 9 + 1 = 15, \quad 1 + 5 = \textbf{6}$$

Now we add up all the single digits that are left.

$$1 + 6 + 6 = \textbf{13}$$

Before reducing this number further to find the Life Path Number, make sure to make a note of it, as this is the **Karmic Debt Number** to one's life – 13 in Henry VIII's case. (More on this to come; see page 129.)

To continue, we add the numbers of 13 together to get:

$$1 + 3 = \mathbf{4}$$

So, King Henry VIII's **Life Path Number** is **4**.

Now it's your turn. Open a journal, and write down your date of birth.

Calculate your Life Path Number using the method outlined, then skip to Chapter 4 to look up your number's meaning. Before you do that, however, you might want to think about how you feel about the number, then check how close your interpretation was to its given meaning.

You will often find that even if you have no experience in numerology, you will have preferences for certain numbers – just like you have preferences for certain types of people.

This doesn't mean that any number is better than the others.

On the contrary; all of them are archetypes of people we meet and learn from throughout our lives.

the FOUR CHALLENGE numbers

These numbers shed light on what lessons we must learn in this life.

It might be four completely different numbers, or some of them could turn out to be the same, depending on the soul contract we came here with.

The **First Challenge Number**
affects us in the first period of our
life, our childhood and adolescence,
sometimes up to our mid-twenties.

The **Second Challenge Number**
overlaps with the First.

It starts in our late teens, and affects
the middle part of our life span,
especially our mid-thirties.

The **Third Challenge Number** affects us throughout our life. You could think of this as the Main Lesson.

The **Fourth Challenge Number** affects us in later life, in old age.

To calculate your Challenge Numbers, you must use **subtraction**.

Once again, let's take King Henry VIII's birth date as an example.

First, we reduce all numbers to
single digits, just as we did previously,
with the Life Path Number (see pages
32–36).

28 June 1491

becomes:

1 (day) **6** (month) **6** (year)

To calculate the First Challenge Number, we need to find the difference between the numbers representing the **day** and the **month**, so, in this case,

1 and **6**

Henry's **First Challenge Number** is:

6 − 1 = **5**

To calculate the Second Challenge Number, find the difference between the numbers representing the **day** and the **year**, so, in this case,

1 and **6**

Henry's **Second Challenge Number** is:

$$6 - 1 = 5$$

Now, to calculate the Third Challenge Number, find the difference between the **First** and **Second Challenge Numbers**, in this case,

5 and **5**

Henry's **Third Challenge Number** is:

$5 - 5 = 0$

To calculate the Fourth Challenge
Number, find the difference between
the numbers representing the **month**
and the **year**, so, in this case,

6 and **6**

Henry's **Fourth Challenge Number** is:

$$6 - 6 = 0$$

As you can see from this example, it is possible to have two or more Challenge Numbers match.

This reinforces the importance of that lesson, and foretells intense opportunities to learn it.

As we can see from Henry VIII's Third and Fourth Challenge Numbers, it is also possible to arrive at 0 as a Challenge Number, when two numbers are the same in your birth date. This will act as a substitute 9, as it is mathematically impossible to have 9 as a Challenge Number.

For this reason, you will find the Challenge Number 0 listed under 9 in Chapter 4 (page 117) describing number meanings.

CHAPTER

CORE
NUMBERS
based on the NAME

Nomen est omen, "the name is a sign", say the ancients.

It is true; so much so, that there are three Core Numbers, and their minors, to be derived from one's name. These are the **Expression**, the **Minor Expression**, the **Soul Urge**, the **Minor Soul Urge**, the **Personality** and the **Minor Personality Numbers**.

Your name carries the key to your personality, and the knowledge and history your soul has gathered and been through before it arrived into your current body.

Of course, there are some exceptions, like names changed because of adoption, or dead names of trans people.

If you have changed your name because of marriage, adoption, gender transition, or any other reason, and you identify with and use your new name exclusively, please use this name instead of your birth name.

Using the birth name would be ideal, but only if you think about yourself using that name. Even if you don't use it anymore, you could still calculate your numbers based on it, to see how things have shifted since the change in your identity.

Nicknames or artists' aliases do not count as changes. Those will be taken into account in the Minor Numbers, however.

REMEMBER:
ALWAYS USE THE NAME YOU IDENTIFY WITH.

the EXPRESSION
number

This number is also called the
Destiny Number.

It reveals the person's life goal, their
priorities, and their potential regarding
talents and shortcomings.

How resonant this number is depends on how well the person taps into these possibilities, and how well they handle their negative traits.

Use your full name, as it appears in your passport, including any middle names, but leave out any titles (like Dr or Mrs) as well as any suffixes (like Jr or 'VIII' in Henry's case).

Using the chart on page 25, calculate the Expression Number by adding up the value of **every letter** in your name.

Let's take Henry VIII for example.

His birth name is Henry Tudor. We do not use the number 8 here, even though that is how the world knows him today.

We will use that name for calculating the Minor Expression Number (on page 64).

H E N R Y

$8 + 5 + 5 + 9 + 7 = \mathbf{34}$

$3 + 4 = \mathbf{7}$

T U D O R

$2 + 3 + 4 + 6 + 9 = \mathbf{24}$

$2 + 4 = \mathbf{6}$

Now we've got each name down
to a single digit, we add the values
together and continue until we get
to a single digit again, so:

$7 + 6 = \mathbf{13}$,

$1 + 3 = \mathbf{4}$

So, Henry VIII's **Expression Number**
is **4**.

Just like with the Life Path Number, make sure you calculate each name separately first, and reduce them to their single-digit forms, to allow special numbers to emerge.

Here we have the Karmic Debt Number 13 (see page 129) for the king to overcome, which, interestingly, was the same one we found in his Life Path Number.

the MINOR
EXPRESSION
number

As the title indicates, whilst this number on its own has a minor influence, the Minor Expression Number does add nuance to your Expression Number.

For this number we calculate the **values of each letter** in the name everyone knows you by, or the one you use with your close relations.

So, for example, Kathleen becomes Kat, Madonna Louise Ciccone becomes simply Madonna, Henry Tudor becomes Henry VIII (just "8" for our purposes).

The Minor Expression Number compensates for any shortcomings in the main Expression Number.

You will often find that numbers are present in this name that are missing in your official name, or that certain numbers are reinforced.

H E N R Y

$8 + 5 + 5 + 9 + 7 = \mathbf{34}$

$3 + 4 = \mathbf{7}$

Now we need to add the VIII ("8" in this case), so we get:

$7 + 8 = \mathbf{15}$,

$1 + 5 = \mathbf{6}$

So, Henry VIII's **Minor Expression Number** is **6**.

the SOUL URGE
number

This number is also called the Hearts Desire Number.

It reveals your hopes and dreams and influences everything we do.

The Soul Urge Number is calculated using only the **vowels** of your full name.

Vowels are usually straightforward: anything that can be pronounced with one, long breath is a vowel.

A, **E**, **I**, **O**, **U** are always vowels.

note:

As already mentioned earlier, the only tricky letter is Y.

In general, Y is considered a vowel if it is the only vowel in the syllable (Bryan, Lynn) or when it is used as an "I" or an "E" sound, as in Yvonne, or Henry.

So, the only vowels in "HENRY"
are E and Y, which means:

$$5 + 7 = \mathbf{12},$$
$$1 + 2 = \mathbf{3}$$

For "TUDOR", it's U and O, which is:

$$3 + 6 = \mathbf{9}$$

Now we add those together and
continue until we get to a single digit:

$$3 + 9 = \mathbf{12},$$
$$1 + 2 = \mathbf{3}$$

So, Henry VIII's **Soul Urge Number** is **3**.

the MINOR SOUL URGE
number

This number gives nuance to what you really want in life, and how much you might limit yourself in achieving your dreams and potential. It is calculated by adding up the values of the **vowels** in your nickname or alias.

H **E** N R **Y** 8

$$5 + 7 = \mathbf{12},$$
$$1 + 2 = \mathbf{3} + \mathbf{8} = \mathbf{11}$$

The number 11 is a **master number** (see page 122). We don't reduce Master Numbers with the Minor Numbers, so Henry VIII's **Minor Soul Urge Number** is **11**.

How fascinating to see that as a normal (although royal) person he had normal numbers, but as a king, he has a Master Number as his Soul Urge!

the PERSONALITY
number

Like its name suggests, the Personality Number shows us the persona we show to the outside world. This is the side others see of you, and what you show when you first meet people.

This number is calculated by adding up all the **consonants** in your name. Consonants are straightforward: anything that you can't draw out like a vowel, is a consonant.

The only tricky one, again, is Y.

Y is a consonant when its pronunciation is dependent on a vowel, like in Brittney or Taylor, or when it acts as a soft J sound, like in Yasmin or Yusuf.

As you get to know someone more closely, you will show them more – your Soul Urge Number will come more into the picture, along with your other numbers.

So, the consonants in HENRY are H, N and R, so we get:

H E **N R** Y

8 + 5 + 9 = **22**

2 + 2 = **4**

In TUDOR, the consonants are
T, D and R, so we get:

T U **D** O **R**

2 + 4 + 9 = **15**

1 + 5 = **6**

Now we add up the value of the two
names:

4 + 6 = **10**,
1 + 0 = **1**

Henry VIII's **Personality Number** is **1**.

the MINOR PERSONALITY
number

The Minor Personality Number adds nuance to the major one, and sheds light on aspects of your personality that you are comfortable with, or that you can easily tap into.

This number is calculated by adding up the values of consonants in your nickname or alias.

H E **N R** Y
$8 + 5 + 9 = \mathbf{22}, \quad 2 + 2 = \mathbf{4}$

Now we add the VIII suffix, just "8" here, to get:

$$4 + 8 = \mathbf{12},$$
$$1 + 2 = \mathbf{3}$$

Henry VIII's **Minor Personality Number** is **3**.

These are the Core Numbers that can be derived from your birth date and name.

These show the most important, most defining aspects of you as a human being.

It is interesting to compare your Core Numbers, to see if you have any patterns.

If you have repeating numbers, those aspects and lessons are more prominent than others, and require more consideration.

King Henry VIII's
Core Numbers are:

Life Path Number

4

Expression Number

4

Minor Expression Number

6

Soul Urge Number

3

Minor Soul Urge Number

11

Personality Number

1

Minor Personality Number

3

As you can see, Henry has two 3s, which indicates a strong desire for enjoyment, entertainment, friends and an active social life. He also has a Master Number in a Minor position, which indicates a connection to religion and a desire for peace and stability.

Thinking about why King Henry VIII founded the Church of England, the connection between his Soul Urge Number 3 and his Minor Soul Urge Number 11 makes complete sense.

The Catholic Church does not recognize divorce, and there was no such thing as a civil divorce back in King Henry VIII's time. For this reason, King Henry VIII created the Church of England, a Christian church that is independent from the Vatican.

Appointing himself as the head of the church, he was able to divorce his first wife Catherine of Aragon, on the basis of her not being able to give him a male heir.

CHAPTER

4

NUMBER
MEANINGS

Each number has a general meaning
that is adjusted according to the
position it appears in.

These meanings are very intuitive,
and with a little practice you will have
a feel for how the meanings change
slightly with their position.

Refer to this chart for a quick guide
to interpreting numbers in different
positions.

Life Path Number

This is the broad blueprint of your life.

Challenge Number

This is a thing you will struggle with.

Expression Number

This is your goal and potential in life.

Soul Urge Number

This is what you want deep down
in your soul, your motivation for
your actions.

Personality Number

This is what you want others to see
of you.

Let's take the **number 1** for example.

As a **Life Path Number**, it shows a great leader who will likely have that role to fill in their life.

As a **Challenge Number**, it shows someone who struggles to stand up for themselves and step into their power.

As an **Expression Number**, it shows someone who works hard to become more confident and to live up to their role in life.

As a **Soul Urge Number**, it shows an extremely driven, active person who knows what they want and will, more likely than not, get it.

As a **Personality Number**, it shows a self-confident, inspiring person.

The following keywords will give a little nuance to the numbers, which you will be able to enhance for yourself when you start to analyse your and others' charts.

Positive attributes:

- Leader
- Effective
- Determined
- Persistent
- Courageous
- Innovative

Negative attributes:

- Selfish
- Controlling
- Dominating
- Aggresive
- Tyrannical

This number corresponds to:

- The **magician** and the **aces** in the Tarot
- The Zodiac sign of **leo**
- The colours **gold** and **orange**
- The birth days **1**, **10**, **19** and **28**

Positive attributes:

- Peaceful
- Perceptive
- Empathetic
- Diplomatic
- Refined
- Sensual
- Inclusive

Negative attributes:

- Over-sensitive
- Secretive
- Vindictive

This number corresponds to:

- The **high priestess** and the **twos** in the Tarot
- The Zodiac sign of **cancer**
- The colours **white** and **pearl**
- The birth days **2**, **11**, **20** and **29**

Positive attributes:

- Creative
- Artistic
- Friendly
- Life of the party
- Indulgence
- Optimistic
- Generous

Negative attributes:

- Social butterfly
- Undisciplined
- Cyincal
- Overindulgent

This number corresponds to:

- The **empress** and the **threes** in the Tarot
- The Zodiac sign of **sagittarius**
- The colour **purple**
- The birth days **3**, **12**, **21** and **30**

Positive attributes:

- Dependable
- Down to earth
- Organized
- Just
- Honest
- Ambitious
- Hardworking

4

Negative attributes:

- Blunt
- Judgemental
- Old-fashioned
- Bossy
- Vengeful
- Vigilante

This number corresponds to:

- The **emperor** and the **fours** in the Tarot
- The Zodiac sign of **capricorn**
- The colour **black**
- The birth days **4**, **13**, **22** and **31**

Positive attributes:

- Free soul
- Traveller
- Adventurer
- Curious
- Outgoing
- Positive
- Joyful
- Indulges the senses

Negative attributes:

- Impulsive
- Overindulgent
- Addictions
- Undisciplined
- Uncommitted

This number corresponds to:

- The **hierophant** and the **fives** in the Tarot

- The Zodiac signs of **gemini** and **virgo**

- All **pastel** colours

- The birth days **5**, **14** and **23**

Positive attributes:

- Compassion
- Social activist
- Care giver
- Volunteer
- Responsible
- Love
- Harmonious
- Humble

6

Negative attributes:

- Unsolicited advice
- Interfering
- Martyr
- Saviour complex

This number corresponds to:

- The **lovers** and the **sixes** in the Tarot

- The Zodiac signs of **taurus** and **libra**

- The colours **light blue**, **green** and **turquoise**

- The birth days **6**, **15** and **24**

Positive attributes:

- Spiritual
- Extra senses
- Mystical knowledge
- Solitude
- Independent

Negative attributes:

- Cold
- Unavailable
- Loner
- **Holier**-than-thou
- Egoistic
- Bitter

This number corresponds to:

- The **chariot** and the **sevens** in the Tarot

- The Zodiac sign of **pisces** and **cancer**

- The colours **aquamarine** and **green**

- The birth days **7**, **16** and **25**

8

Positive attributes:

- Leader
- Wealthy
- Business-savvy
- Manager
- Career-focused
- Sensible risk-taker
- Organized
- Powerful

8

Negative attributes:

- Reckless
- Micromanager
- Overpowering
- Show-off
- Unavailable
- Stubborn
- Corrupt

This number corresponds to:

- **Strength** and the **eights** in the Tarot

- The Zodiac signs of **capricorn** and **aquarius**

- All **dark** colours

- The birth days **8**, **17** and **26**

Positive attributes:

- Philanthropist
- Environmentally and socially conscious
- Communicator
- Inspiring
- Imaginative
- Persistent
- Selfless

Negative attributes:

- Mood swings
- Withdrawn
- Uncertain
- Meddling

These numbers correspond to:

- The **hermit** and the **nines** in the Tarot

- The Zodiac signs of **aries** and **scorpio**

- The colour **red**

- The birth days **9**, **18** and **27**

CHAPTER

5

SPECIAL
NUMBERS

There are a few numbers we don't always reduce to single digits. These can be the two master numbers, and the Karmic Debt Numbers, in some cases.

MASTER
NUMBERS

The Master Numbers are **11** and **22**. These are extremely potent, high-energy numbers that came with a big purpose and are usually hard to keep under control in one's life.

They require a special kind of maturity and discipline to achieve their full potential, or they could spiral out of control and into their doom.

This is the number of psychics.

It represents someone who knows things they have no way of knowing, who has a strong connection to the spirit world.

This person might not seem very logical, but more often than not they are right to listen to their gut.

- The **number 11 represents** dreamers who find it easy to inspire others with their vision and charisma.

- They need a goal they can work towards, a larger-than-life plan, otherwise they are prone to depression and anxiety, as well as self-destructive behaviour.

- They find peace in spirituality, rather than materialism and logic.

- They do well in any religion as long as they are left to practice it on their own terms.

This number has all the qualities of numbers 1 and 2, but amplified.

This is the most powerful of all numbers.

People with the number 22 have great potential and can achieve huge successes in whatever field they choose for themselves.

- They are practical, well-organized and ambitious. Real powerhouses of willpower and discipline. Just like 11, 22 can also spiral out of control if they don't find a worthy goal to strive for, and plunge them into addictions and depression.

- It is important for people associated with this number to find a passion that is beyond their personal ambition, and start working for that as early as possible.

- They can move mountains if they can channel their willpower and talent in one, definite direction.

The number 22 has all the qualities of 2 and 4, but amplified.

KARMIC DEBT
NUMBERS

Pythagoras also taught his disciples about metempsychosis – the transmigration of souls after death.

During our many lives we have already lived, we have accumulated a lot of karma; we have lessons to learn, and misdeeds to atone for.

Karmic Debt Numbers suggest there is a lesson we have been unable to learn in a previous life, and that we must learn now.

The Karmic Debt Numbers are **13**, **14**, **16** and **19**, and they are especially important to look out for in the core numbers of your chart. It is to be read together with whatever Core Number it preceded.

When calculating your numbers, always pay attention to the last number before you reduce it into a single-digit one.

For example, if your Expression number adds up to 13, before further reducing it to 4, you must make a note to interpret the Karmic Debt Number 13.

Those with a Karmic Debt
Number of 13
will need to learn self-
discipline, focus and
determination in this life.

- They will face an abundance of obstacles, and if their efforts are not directed towards a single goal, all their efforts will turn out to be futile.

- They are very capable of achieving what they want, if they learn these lessons.

Those with 14 will need
to learn modesty, self-control
and adaptability.

- They will have a roller coaster of a life, and can gain and lose and regain everything they have worked for in an instant.

- Their lesson is to stay calm in the eye of the storm, practice restraint when it comes to the indulgence of the senses, and stay focused on their goals while moving with the ever-changing times.

Those with a Karmic Debt Number of 16 will need to learn humility, and reconnect with their Higher Self, and with Spirit.

- They will face great losses that blow holes in their ego, and lose what they thought they deserved, throughout their life.

- They will have to go through such experiences again and again, until they give up their ego, and find their faith, or they risk ending up bitter and lonely.

Those with a Karmic Debt
Number of 19 will need
to learn independence,
stepping into their power,
and co-operation with
others.

- They will face situations where they
  need to stand up for themselves,
  and stand their ground against
  opposition, even if they are alone
  with their beliefs. This gives them a
  tremendous sense of personal power,
  which can stop them from asking for
  help. This is a big mistake, that can
  lead to isolation and burnout.

- They will need to learn to accept
  (and even ask for) help, and
  collaborate with others to achieve
  their goals.

CHAPTER

6

NUANCE
NUMBERS

While the Core Numbers represent a
person's main, obvious characteristics,
the following numbers add nuance
to them. These are less visible, more
internal qualities that make a person
into who they are – their talents,
shortcomings, and so on.

the KARMIC LESSON CHART

In our journey throughout lives, we have learned many lessons, and we likely have many more to go. There are three numbers to be derived from this chart: the **Karmic Lesson Number**, the **Hidden Passion Number**, and the **Subconscious Self Number**.

To prepare this chart, you have to use your **full name**, like in the Expression Number, but instead of adding up the values of your letters, you have to check which numbers come up, how many times, and which numbers are missing.

Draw a **3-by-3 grid** and label each box with "1s", "2s", "3s", etc., as shown on p. 146.

Now, let's use Henry VIII as an example again to see which numbers his **full name** contains.

So, when we write "Henry Tudor" out in numbers, we get:

H E N R Y
8 5 5 9 7

T U D O R
2 3 4 6 9

Now count how many of each number appear, and note that down in the grid, as shown on the next page.

1s 0	**2**s 1	**3**s 1
4s 1	**5**s 2	**6**s 1
7s 1	**8**s 1	**9**s 2

Let's look at the numbers that can be derived from this chart.

the KARMIC
LESSON number

In contrast to the Karmic Debt
Number, which shows us the lessons
we failed to learn in a previous
incarnation, or the Challenge Numbers,
which show the struggles we will face
and the energies we will need to utilize
and employ to overcome them, the
Karmic Lesson Number helps us find
out which lessons we came here to
learn specifically in this life.

To find your Karmic Lesson Number, you interpret the number, or numbers, that are **missing** from your name.

It is common to have more than one number missing; in these cases, we often find talents that a person is really good at, represented by repeating numbers, which balance the scale.

Henry VIII has the number **1** missing. He came to this world to learn only one lesson: the lesson of being a strong, just leader. If he was successful, this lesson will not show up in the Karmic Debt Numbers in his next life. Remember: learning karmic lessons is an inner process.

Having been a king doesn't necessarily mean he was, or felt like, a strong leader. What we see from the outside and a person's inner life can often be very different.

the HIDDEN PASSION number

This number shows the talent you were born with. If a number is present in your name **two or more times**, you have a hidden talent that, if honed properly through study and practice, could become a big part of your life.

Henry VIII has two 5s and two 9s present in his name, so his **Hidden Passion Numbers** are **5** and **9**.

You can have more than one Hidden Passion Number, or none at all! That is completely fine, too. It doesn't mean you can't be great at anything.

It could mean that your passion might remain a hobby, rather than consuming your life, like we see with famous musicians, or scientists, for example.

the
SUBCONSCIOUS
SELF number

This number shows how you deal
with stress and emergencies, and how
much confidence you have in yourself.

It is once again derived from the Karmic Lesson chart, by **subtracting** the amount of **missing** numbers from 9.

For Henry VIII, this is 9 – 1 = **8**.

Note: If his missing number was 3, you would still be subtracting 1, because we subtract the **amount** of missing numbers, not the actual number that is missing.)

CHAPTER

FURTHER
NUANCE
NUMBERS

the BALANCE
number

The Balance Number shows you the best way you can cope with and mitigate stress.

This is not how you deal with the actual problem, but how you decompress after a stressful situation.

To find your Balance Number, add up the values of your **full name initials**, and reduce them into single digits. Reduce Master Numbers, too.

HENRY **T**UDOR

8 + 2 = 10,

1 + 0 = **1**

Henry VIII's **Balance Number** is **1**.

the MATURITY
number

The Maturity Number shows the revelation people usually experience around the age of 30 to 35. This is your true calling, the moving force of your life.

Once you realize what it is, you'll be able to focus on manifesting this calling, and gradually shed everything surplus that held you back.

To find your Maturity Number, add up your **Expression Number** and your **Life Path Number**, and reduce it to a single digit if necessary. Do not reduce Master Numbers.

Henry VIII's Expression Number is 4, and his Life Path Number is 4, too.

$$4 + 4 = \textbf{8}$$

Henry VIII's **Maturity Number** is **8**.

the RATIONAL
THOUGHT
number

This number shows your way of
thinking, your mindset. Are you a
logical thinker, or do you wear pink
shades at all times? Do you think
outside the box, or do you prefer
tried and tested methods?

To find your Rational Thought
Number, add the value of your **first
name** to the **day** of your birth.

HENRY = **7**

28th = 2 + 8 = 10,
1 + 0 = **1**

7 + 1 = **8**

Henry VIII's **Rational Thought
Number** is **8**.

These are the most important numbers we can derive from our name and date of birth, in order of importance.

You will notice that by the time you are done with your whole chart, most numbers have appeared in one way or the other. This is because, as humans, we are complex creatures with many factors that influence who we are.

These factors also influence each other, creating a fascinating spectrum of the human experience.

It is good to keep in mind that the Core Numbers carry more weight than the Nuance Numbers; to gauge someone's basic personality, it is enough to calculate the Core Numbers.

CHAPTER

the
PROGRESSIVE
CHART

The Progressive chart shows where
you are in your life, which cycle you're
currently running, what kind of forces
influence you at the moment – or will
do so at any given time, if you want to
forecast.

TIMING
with NUMEROLOGY

The most important, and most distinguishable, influences that affect us are the Universal Year, and the Personal Year Numbers.

Just like us, the Earth is going through cycles of nine years, and the energy of these individual years affects us and our progress in life.

The energies ruling the year
numbers are as follows:

1 new beginnings, enthusiasm,
new ideas

2 networking, relationships,
bonding

3 creativity, building, giving birth
(to projects or to a baby)

4 discipline, toil, possibilities

5 refinement, change, risks

 6 serving others, community, family time

7 introspection, self-realization, spiritual growth

 8 reaping what you sowed, reward, success

 9 completion, the end of a cycle, release, closure

the UNIVERSAL YEAR number

This number shows what kind of energies the Earth will face in general. It affects everyone on the planet.

How you react or adapt to it depends on your personal year and your Core Numbers.

To calculate the Universal Year Number, **add up** the digits of the **year**, and reduce them into a **single-digit number**.

Master Numbers are reduced in this case.

For example, 2023 adds up to **7**.

This year brings the opportunity for gaining more awareness about the problems we face and the growing up we need to do as a species.

2024 adds up to **8**, which promises that we will reap what we sowed, and get what we worked for.

the PERSONAL YEAR number

This number shows the influences
specific to you throughout the year.
There is a buffer period of three
months at the end of the year, when
the energy of the previous and the
next year can be felt at the start
and the end of the current year,
respectively.

The height of any given year's energy is around September.

To calculate your Personal Year Number, add up the **day** and **month** of your birth to the **year** you want to find out about.

Let's calculate the personal year number of Henry VIII at the time he was crowned king.

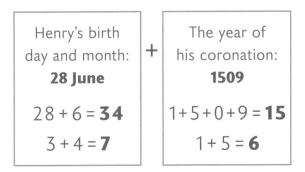

Henry's birth day and month: **28 June**	+	The year of his coronation: **1509**
28 + 6 = **34**		1 + 5 + 0 + 9 = **15**
3 + 4 = **7**		1 + 5 = **6**

7 + **6** = 13

1 + 3 = **4**

So, Henry VIII's **Personal Year Number** is **4**.

Henry VIII's Personal Year Number was 4 when he was crowned.

An interesting correspondence is that in Tarot, number 4 is the **Emperor** card.

Knowing the year's numbers helps in planning ahead, or thinking about the past retrospectively.

For example, 1945, the year the Second World War ended, was a Universal Year 9, and brought closure to a horrible period for mankind.

CHAPTER

TIMING and FORECASTING

If you're wondering when would be the best time to launch a new project, propose to your beloved, or leave the job you hate, take advantage of numerology.

Each day carries a different energy, so it makes sense to calculate the energy most suited to your goal.

A date with the number 9 is perfect for giving in your resignation, a 1 day is well suited to start a new business, and a 6 day would be beneficial for proposals and marriages.

To see a specific date's energies, all you have to do is add up the numbers of the complete date: day, month, and year, just like you'd do for a Life Path Number.

You need to reduce Master Numbers to single digits in this case, too.

Seeing only the day's energy is helpful,
but remember, the energy of 1 May
is quite different to the energy of
1 September, and if you change the
year, that is a whole different cup of
tea entirely.

It is therefore always best to check the
whole date.

Let's pick a date in the future:

29 April 2029

It adds up to **1***, which means this will be a good day to start new projects, invest in something new, follow your ideas and begin manifesting them.

* 29 (2 + 9 = 11, 1 + 1) = **2**
   April = **4**
   2049 = (2 + 0 + 4 + 9 = 15,
                1 + 5) = **4**
   2 + 4 + 4 = **10**,
   1 + 0 = **1**

If you wanted to launch your new website selling hand-made creations, this would be an ideal day to do it.

The day before, 28 April 2029, adds up to 9, which means it is a good day to end the old, clean up after it, so you are ready to welcome the new.

Similarly, 30 April 2029 adds up to 2, which means it will be a good day to spend with family and friends, or to look for partners and do some networking for the new business.

The possibility of a successful launch is supported by 2029's Universal Year Number 4, as 4 carries the energy of opportunities and hard work in it.

EVENT NAME

Another method is to use an Event Name in the calculations.

An Event Name is a short description of the event that you want to forecast, such as "Wedding", or "Business Launch".

You calculate your own **Life Path Number**, then the **Event Name's Expression Number**, just like you would for a person's name, and see which day suits these best by looking for these numbers in the future.

Looking for a suitable date seems daunting, but you don't have to calculate it by yourself. There are many apps and software available that will do it for you in seconds.

Event example

Suppose Henry VIII wants to open a Marriage Counselling Office.

We take his **Life Path Number**, **4**.

Then, we name this event, say,

"Counselling Office Opening".

Don't worry about the naming. Whatever name you choose, it will be meaningful to you, therefore carry your energy within it.

We calculate the **Event Name's Expression Number**, which in this case is **3**.

And finally, we look for a **date in the future** that carries beneficial energies for this event – days with 3 and 4 in their numbers.

REMEMBER:

The key to learning numerology is practice.

Prepare your own chart, and the charts of those around you, those of celebrities and famous historical people, to see how number combinations manifest in a wide variety of personalities and destinies.

I wish you every success on your journey learning and using numerology.

May you find the best version of yourself through the numbers, and may they bring health, wealth and joy into your life!